The Welsh Coast

KU-524-159

ACC. No: 02735668

N

Isle of Anglesey

Dee Estuary

Llandudno

Holyhead

Conwy

Flint

Caernarfon

Lleyn Peninsula

Harlech

Aberystwyth

Aberaeron

New Quay

St David's

St Bride's Bay

Pembroke

Swansea

Newport

Carmarthen Bay

Cardiff

Gower Peninsula

The Welsh Coast

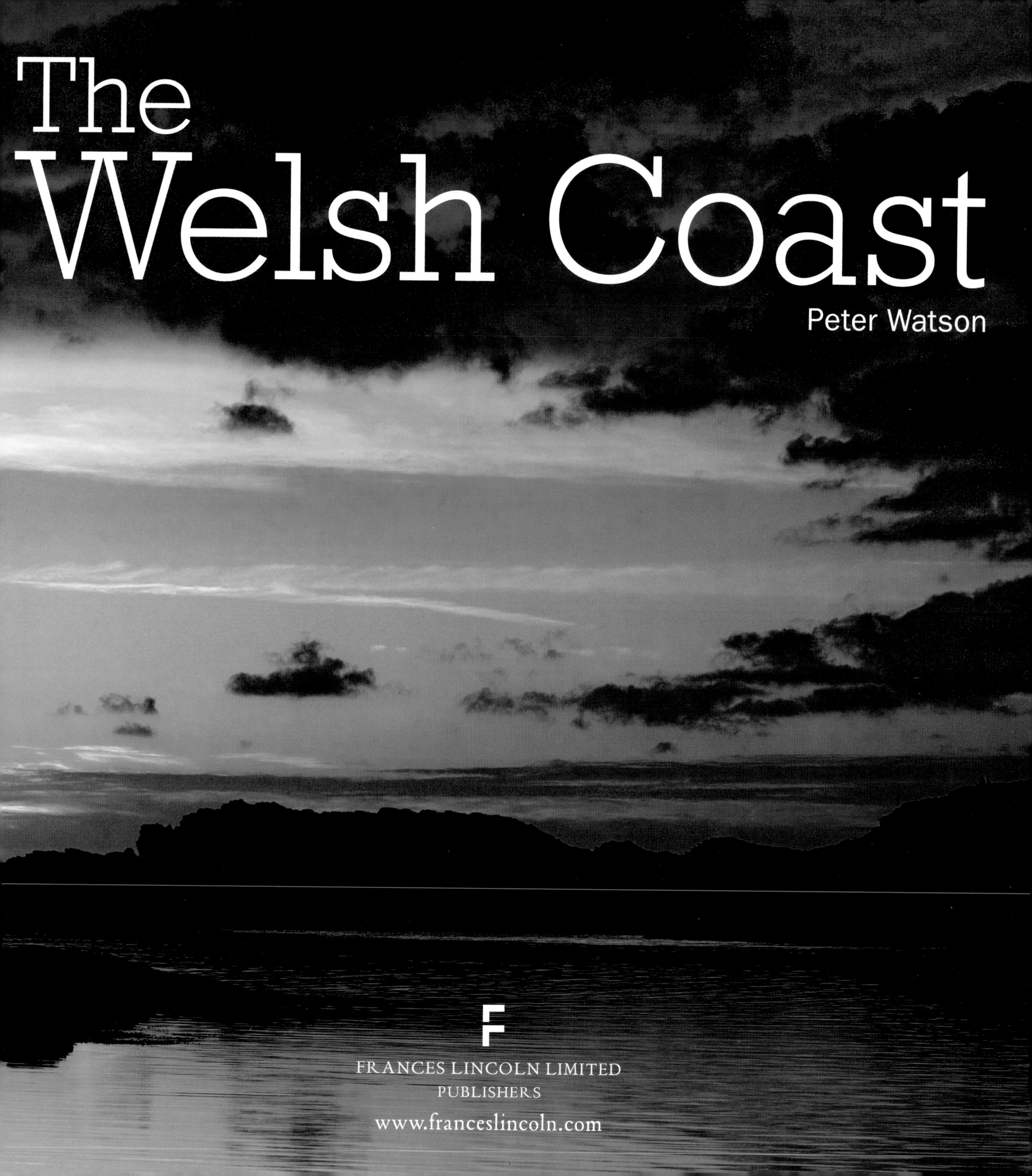

The Welsh Coast

Peter Watson

F

FRANCES LINCOLN LIMITED
PUBLISHERS
www.franceslincoln.com

Frances Lincoln Limited
4 Torriano Mews
Torriano Avenue
London NW5 2RZ
www.franceslincoln.com

The Welsh Coast
Copyright © Frances Lincoln Limited 2010
Text and photographs copyright © Peter Watson 2010
First Frances Lincoln edition 2010

Peter Watson has asserted his right to be identified
as the author of this work in accordance with the
Copyright, Designs and Patents Act 1988 (UK).

All rights reserved.
No part of this publication may be reproduced,
stored in a retrieval system, or transmitted, in any
form, or by any means, electrical, mechanical,
photocopying, recording or otherwise without the
prior written permission of the publisher or a
licence permitting restricted copying. In the United
Kingdom such licences are issued by the Copyright
Licensing Agency, Saffron House, 6–10 Kirby Street,
London EC1N 8TS.

A catalogue record for this book is available from the
British Library.

ISBN 9780711231115

Printed and bound in China

9 8 7 6 5 4 3 2 1

PAGE 1 Barafundle Bay, Pembrokeshire
PAGES 2–3 Trearddur Bay, Anglesey
THIS PAGE Freshwater West, Pembrokeshire
FOLLOWING PAGES Horton Beach, Gower Peninsula

Contents

Introduction

As a photographer I am drawn to Wales. This might, of course, come as no surprise, but I should immediately add that, attractive as they undoubtedly are, it is not only the mountains, hills and valleys that lure me to this majestic landscape: it is also the coastline. This is because here, at the meeting point of sky, water and land, there exists a mesmerizing fusion of stillness and movement which I can honestly say is as close to poetry in motion as anything I can imagine. I am happy to admit that I find it all most compelling. I think my fascination is due to the beguiling elements that can be found along the length of the coastline and, like many other photographers, I seek out these features and endeavour to thrive upon their stunning visual attributes. If you then add in the unique quality of coastal light, you have all the ingredients necessary to whet the appetite of not only photographers and painters but also the more casual observer. And the reason for this is simple: the more you see, the more you want to see.

The coast is where there is space, solitude and a connection with a timeless, unspoilt world that is becoming increasingly difficult to find. This is no doubt why a visit to our shores is, for many, a form of escape. As a photographer it is, for me, also a challenge. My motivation and primary objective are always to capture those fleeting, magical moments when everything falls miraculously into place to produce a flawless display of nature's regal magnificence. Sadly, such occasions are by no means a regular occurrence and, frustratingly, they are also quite unpredictable. I've lost count of the number of times I have visited a location, day after relentless day, only to be thwarted by unexpected rain, an unfavourable sky or perhaps a rogue cloud trespassing across the horizon to impede my light. I have then been forced to return home, deflated, dejected and with absolutely nothing to show for my efforts. But it's not all doom and gloom, because there have also been moments of sheer ecstasy – and I do not use this word lightly, believe me; these are the moments photographers crave – when the basic elements of light, land, sky and water suddenly – and perhaps only for a split second –

excel themselves to become precious elements. Like sparkling jewels, they irradiate and transform the landscape into a masterpiece of colours, textures, shapes and patterns.

I invite you to share some of those cherished moments and accompany me as I travel through the nooks and crannies of the twisting and endlessly varied Welsh coast. Starting at the northern tip, the birdwatcher's paradise along the Dee Estuary, we pause at some of the landmarks and then head west to make the relatively short trip to the Isle of Anglesey, passing along the way the resorts of Rhyl, Colwyn Bay and Llandudno. From here we go to the Lleyn Peninsula, which leads us to the expansive stretch of coastline from Tremadog all the way down to Cardigan Bay. The next stop is the renowned Pembrokeshire Coast National Park and then we go on to the equally impressive Gower Peninsula. Our coastal odyssey ends on a high note with an exploration of some of the beaches and bays that can be found hidden away between the bustling cities of Swansea and Cardiff.

From castles in the sand to castles on a cliff top, the Welsh coast is as beautiful and dramatic as it is diverse, and there are many visual delights to be savoured throughout the journey. It has a unique character, which I have attempted to portray in the photographs that follow. You will see that I have, from time to time, strayed off the beaten path a little. My wanderings are a result of my desire to create a series of pictures that are more than a collection of 'postcard' images. Sometimes, therefore, the more familiar locations have taken a back seat to some of the less visited, often overlooked, places which in my opinion deserve to be given greater recognition.

Producing this book has not been without its challenges, but it has been a deeply rewarding experience and there have been many unforgettable moments which I will always treasure. I hope that, as you browse through the pages, you too will share my lasting enjoyment of the Welsh coastal adventure.

Peter Watson

The Dee Estuary to Caernarvon Bay

PREVIOUS PAGES *Evening sky* **The Dee Estuary**
Located along the northern tip of Wales, the Dee Estuary is one of Britain's most
important birding locations. Water levels have declined sharply over the years
and much of the estuary has become silted. However, the combination of tidal
waters, sand, mud and marshland is the perfect environment for wetland and
shore birds, though it is a little more challenging for wingless creatures.

LEFT *Sand pattern, early morning sunlight* **The Dee Estuary**

ABOVE *Mudflats* **The Dee Estuary**
The power of photography becomes apparent in this abstract study of what would
normally be a rather mundane, even unattractive, coastal feature. When you move
in close and isolate a section of it, a stretch of mud becomes a mini-landscape,
a rich tapestry of colour and texture and a worthy subject for the camera.

ABOVE *Incoming tide* **Near Llandulas**
There is always something to photograph at the coast,
even on a dull, cloudy day. Here a long shutter speed
captures the ephemeral quality of the incoming tide.

RIGHT *Horizon light* **Llandudno Pier**
Standing at a rather impressive 2,295ft/700m, Llandudno Pier
is the longest in Wales and the fifth longest in England and
Wales. Originally constructed in 1858 it was rebuilt in 1877 as
an integral part of the development of Llandudno as a seaside
resort. It is now a Grade II listed building and is regarded by
many as one of the finest remaining Victorian piers in Britain.

ABOVE Fading light across the promenade **Llandudno, Gwynedd**

RIGHT Low tide, low cloud **Rhos on Sea, Clwyd**

ABOVE *Talacre Lighthouse* **Point of Ayr**
When I researched the Point of Ayr (the northernmost point of mainland Wales) I was surprised to discover that it was the site of a productive coal mine until as recently as 1996. There is now no evidence of the mine's existence and to look at the area you would think it had never been anything more than an empty stretch of beach and sand dunes. It is a pity the site has been so comprehensively cleared, because old, disused buildings are always interesting to photograph.

RIGHT *Groyne detail* **Near Llandulas**

OPPOSITE *Winter sunlight over a rugged coastline*
Near Colwyn Bay

ABOVE *Majestic light* **Conway Castle**

Conway is, in my opinion (shared by others), one of the finest and most impressive
castles in Wales. Commanding an elevated position, with its eight imposing towers
and well-preserved surrounding wall it is a majestic sight. Constructed between 1283
and 1289 by the English monarch Edward I, the castle oozes medieval atmosphere.
Perched proudly on a rock promontory above its small town (the monument's
irregular design follows the shape of its rocky base), it was perfectly positioned
to repel raiders and guard the entrance to the River Conway and the town's harbour.
Just as spectacular as the castle are the views from its battlements of the surrounding
mountains, sea and countryside, particularly on days of good visibility.

Standing virtually on the border with England, Flint Castle was built towards the end of the thirteenth century, close to the River Dee – so close, in fact, that at high tide the river filled the castle's moat and ships were able to berth at an adjacent dock. The course of the Dee has changed dramatically over the centuries and now the castle stands on a hilltop overlooking vast stretches of sand, mud and marshland. Although the building is now ruined, its original outline and design can still be seen and the parts that remain appear to be well preserved. Originally the castle had an inner ward and, separated by the moat, an outer bailey. In the eighteenth century it was used as the county jail and this use continued until as recently as the 1960s (which is surprising in view of its present condition).

BELOW *St Baglan's Church* **Llanfaglan**
The ancient church stands alone in a gloriously isolated position in the middle of a field overlooking Caernarvon Bay. An attractive sky and the last light of the day helped me to portray its romantic setting.

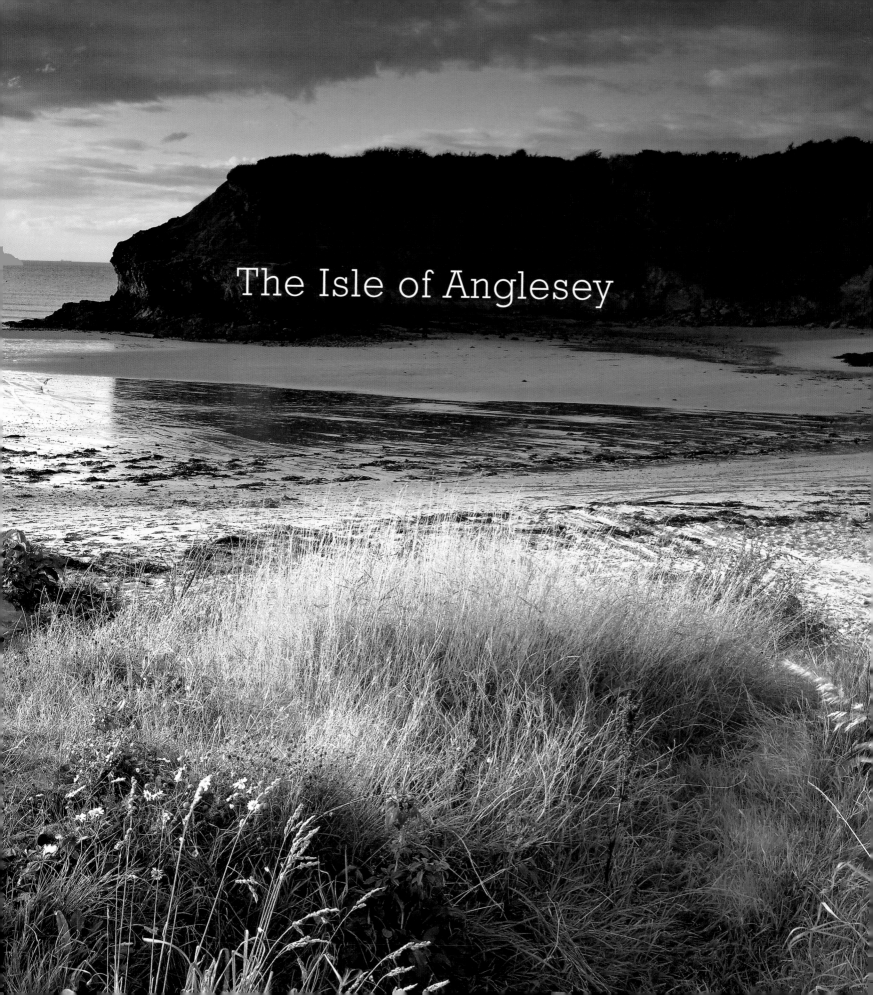

The Isle of Anglesey

PREVIOUS PAGES *Deserted beach* **Cemaes Bay**

ABOVE *Pebbled beach, gentle tide* **Lligwy Bay**

ABOVE *A bracing winter morning* **Porth Trecastell**

LEFT ABOVE *Late evening sunlight across the harbour* **Cemaes Bay**

Enjoying a peaceful position along the northern tip of Anglesey, Cemaes Bay looks north across the Irish Sea. Along with Amlwch, the village benefited from the large source of copper mined from nearby Parys Mountain and shipbuilding became a major industry in the nineteenth century. Good local beaches and safe bathing have ensured that Cemaes Bay remains a popular destination for visitors to the island.

LEFT BELOW *The old harbour* **Amlwch**

In the eighteenth century the world's largest source of copper was found close to Amlwch on Parys Mountain. The volumes of copper being exported were such that the village grew to become an important port with 5,000 inhabitants. Its expansion was also boosted by the development of other industries, including shipbuilding. Of particular interest is the harbour, which retains an atmosphere evocative of earlier times.

RIGHT *A cluster of cottages* **Moelfre**

Although the name of Moelfre can be traced back to the twelfth century, the village itself is relatively new. It became established as recently as the early 1900s, although it lies at the centre of an area rich in historical monuments and ruins. Many are within walking distance of the village, including a twelfth-century chapel at Lligwy, the Cromlech, an ancient burial chamber, and Din Lligwy, a settlement that is thought to date back to the Iron Age.

LEFT ABOVE *Avenue of pebbles* **Church Bay**

LEFT BELOW *Two caves, countless boulders* **Church Bay**
I have visited the Isle of Anglesey many times
and thought I knew every part of its coastline. It was
therefore a pleasant surprise to discover this quiet
and secluded bay. Photographically speaking it is
without doubt one of the most interesting and intriguing
beaches on the island. It has a unique geology, which
is the perfect raw material for image making.

RIGHT *Abstract expression* **Porth Trecastell**

Coastal tapestry **Bull Bay**

Bull Bay is the most northerly village in Wales. However, I was
more interested in its beach than its location. Low tide reveals it
to be an intricate tapestry of eye-catching shapes, textures and
colours, and I spent a happy hour combing the bay for images.

Isolated cottages **Porth Nobla**

The grand finale **Aberffraw**
St Cwyfan's Church, also known as the Church in the Sea, is situated on a
small tidal island, close to the mainland near the village of Aberffraw. Dating
back to the thirteenth century, the church is still in use, mainly for christenings
and weddings. Already in an attractive setting, the location of the ancient
building was, at the time of my taking the photograph, further enhanced by the
exquisite twilight and sky. If only all days could end with such a grand finale.

Sea mist, sinking sun **South Stack Lighthouse**
South Stack Lighthouse takes its name from the small island on which it
stands. Situated off the north-west coast of Anglesey, it was built in 1809,
although permission for its construction was originally sought in 1665
and the petition was refused by Charles II. The lighthouse is still in use
today and for the past 200 years it has ensured safe passage for ships
crossing the Irish Sea between Holyhead, Dublin and Liverpool.

ABOVE *Evening, late summer* **Penmon Priory**

Penmon Priory lies in a peaceful corner of Anglesey along the coast 4 miles/6.5 kilometres
north-east of Beaumaris. The original monastery was founded in the sixth century by St Seiriol
but was later destroyed by Viking raiders and then rebuilt during the Norman period.
The priory is part of a group of historic buildings, which include St Seiriol's Church, a
dovecote and the Holy Well of St Seiriol. The dovecote is particularly notable and a fine
example of this type of structure, with the capacity to accommodate about a thousand birds.

RIGHT *The joy of autumn* **Newborough Warren**

The island of Anglesey has an extensive and diverse coastline. In addition to its varied
and complex geology the island has one of Britain's largest dune systems at Newborough
Warren. There are also mudflats, a saltmarsh and an extensive forest, as well, of course, as
several miles of golden sands. My visit coincided with the peak of autumn and I was therefore
lured to the area where the forest and sand dunes meet. This stretch of coastline is bursting
with life and it was a joy to wander through its colourful pathways and capture its beauty.

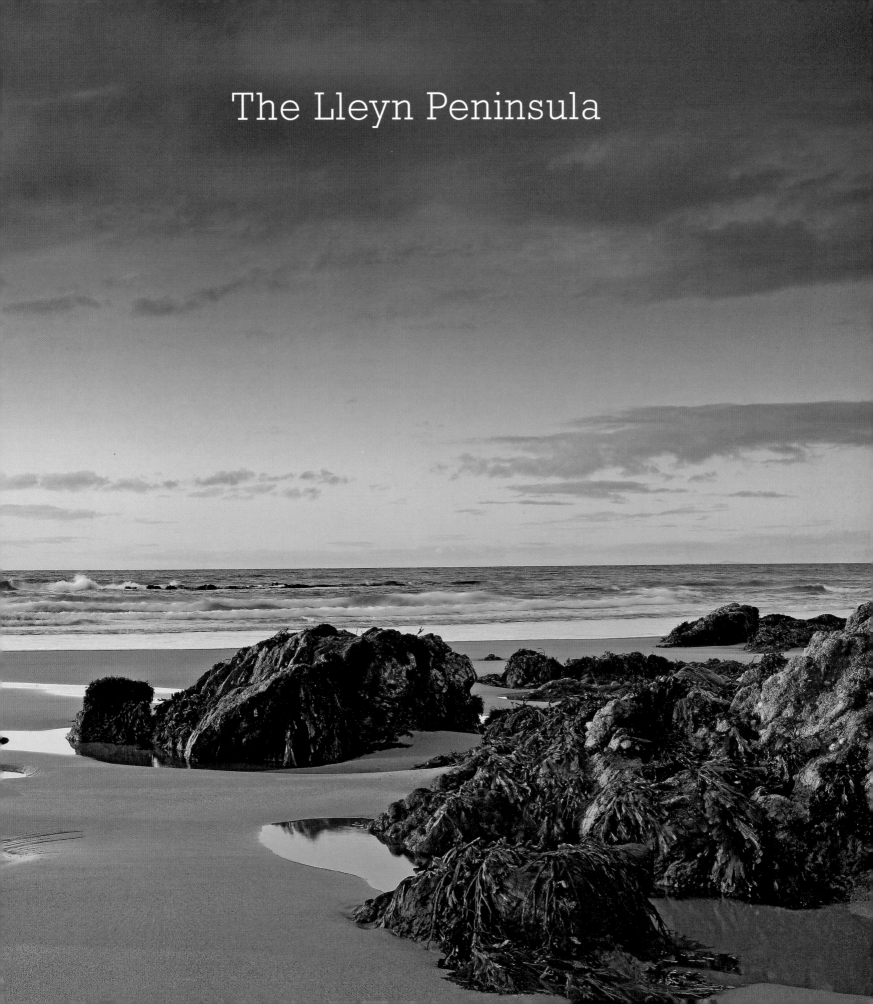

The Lleyn Peninsula

PREVIOUS PAGES *Winter sunset* **Porth Towyn**

LEFT *Evanescent waves* **Aberdesach**
Timing was critical in the making of this photograph and not
only because of the light. My objective was to catch the waves at
the optimum moment as they washed over the rocky foreground.
I made several attempts before being satisfied with the result.

ABOVE *Last light of the day* **Porth Ysglaig**

ABOVE *A bracing February day* **Porth Nefyn**

RIGHT *Incoming tide* **Trefor**

BELOW *Calm water reflections* **Abersoch**
The old harbour is evidence of the village's origins as a fishing port. Nowadays, however, it is mainly yachts and dinghies that are moored there because Abersoch, thanks to the area's mild climate and suitability for water sports, has become a popular holiday resort. The village boasts a long row of colourful beach huts, which are much sought after and, as a result, change hands for exceptionally high prices. They are also a joy to photograph and fortunately no great financial outlay is necessary in order to enjoy their visual delights!

RIGHT *Harbour view* **Abersoch**

PREVIOUS PAGES *Deserted beach, February* **Criccieth**
Criccieth Castle is one of the later fortresses to be built, not being constructed until the early part of the thirteenth century. Perched in an elevated position on a rocky headland, the castle overlooks the sea and the views from it extend as far as Snowdonia in the north to Harlech Castle to the south-east. At the time the castle was built Criccieth was a tiny village, consisting of just a few houses and a church. In medieval times it was known as Treferthyr (Martyr's Town) and today the local primary school is still known as Ysgol Treferthyr. In 1867 the introduction of the Cambrian Coast Railway helped the town gain popularity as a Victorian seaside resort. It gradually expanded to its present size of approximately two thousand people and today it remains a popular and unspoilt holiday destination.

ABOVE *The harbour* **Porth Dinllaen**
Approximately two dozen cottages, small buildings and huts are grouped above the harbour to form the tiny hamlet of Porth Dinllaen. It is now owned by the National Trust and access by car is restricted to permit holders. Most visitors trek across the beach from Morfa Nefyn, which is what I did – several times. For some reason my camera and tripod seemed to gain weight with each journey.

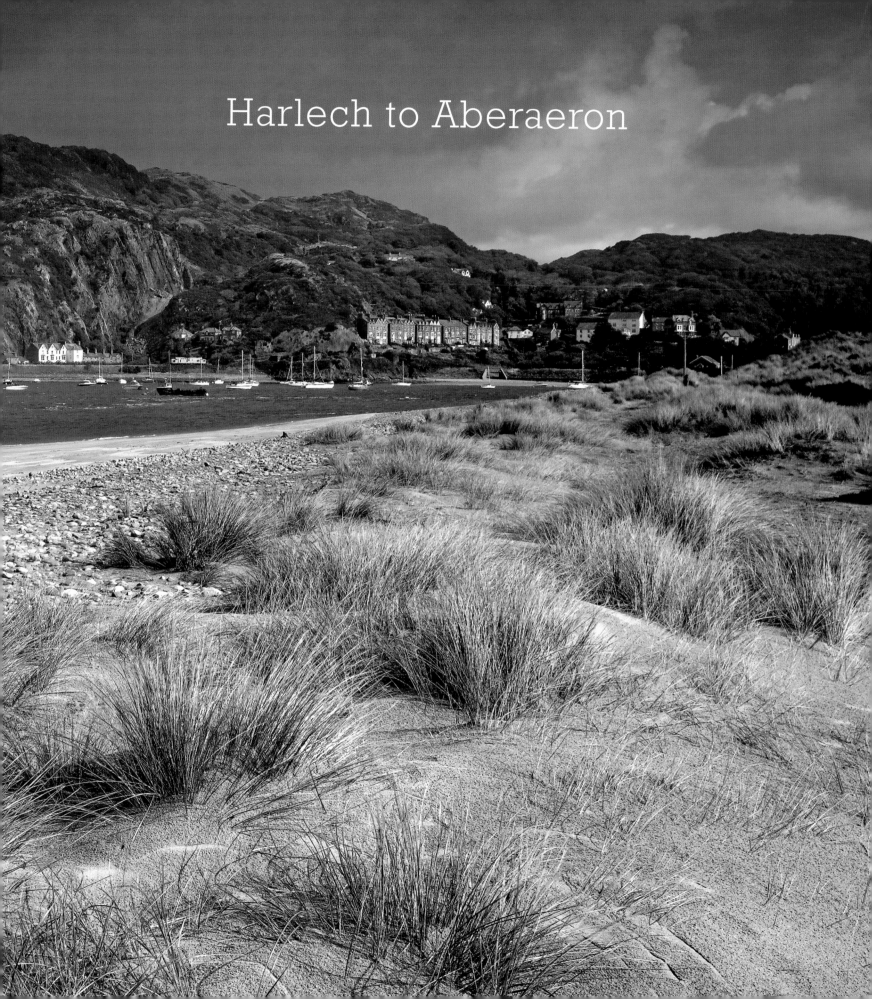

Harlech to Aberaeron

PREVIOUS PAGES *Barmouth viewed from the south bank of the bay* **Barmouth Bay**

ABOVE *A quiet winter morning* **Barmouth**
Lying between a towering mountain range and a broad sweep of golden
coastline, Barmouth has, since Victorian times, been a popular holiday
destination. Like any seaside resort the town becomes crowded during the
summer months and for this reason I prefer to visit during the quieter seasons.
Give me a cold, bracing winter day, a deserted beach and a few glimpses of
soft, gentle sunlight, and I will play happily with my camera for hours on end.

BELOW *The harbour* **Aberaeron**

Once a tiny fishing village, Aberaeron expanded early in the nineteenth century with the development of its harbour at the mouth of the Aeron River. The town still retains its Georgian elegance, particularly around the harbour, where there are fine examples of Regency-style buildings. Edward Haycock, the architect credited with the design of the town, was heavily influenced by John Nash, whose architecture can be seen in the historic city of Bath. Closer to hand is Llanerchaeron, a Nash-designed mansion now under the management of the National Trust. Built between 1794 and 1796, it has remained virtually unaltered and is one of the best examples of the architect's early work.

BELOW *A silent guardian* **Barmouth**
Groynes are a common feature of the coastline and play an essential role
in the preservation of our beaches; however, important as they are, these
wooden structures are, to my eye, much more than mere silent guardians
of our shores. They are a treasure trove of weathered colours and textures,
a cornerstone on which I can build many coastal images. Groynes are
one of my most highly regarded visual aids and I am deeply thankful
for their existence. Long may they continue to watch over our coast.

ABOVE *Low tide in Cardigan Bay* **Aberystwyth**
The expansion of the Cambrian Railway line accelerated the development
of Aberystwyth as a popular holiday destination. The town is considerably
larger than neighbouring resorts and because of this it has never been
totally reliant on tourism. It has also gained a reputation as an important
centre of education since the University College of Wales was established
there in 1872. This has now been replaced by the highly regarded
Aberystwyth University. One of the Victorian attractions was re-created in
1985, when one of the world's largest camera obscuras was completed.
Located next to the town on Constitution Hill, the device projects images of
the surrounding landscape over a great distance with remarkable clarity.

Looking towards the Lleyn Peninsula **Llandanwg**
There is an old, disused church on the coast at
Llandanwg and, having a penchant for ancient buildings
(the older and more dilapidated the better), I visited
the beach late one February afternoon. On arrival my
initial reaction was one of disappointment, because the
church was virtually buried in sand dunes and there
was almost nothing I could photograph. But all was
not lost, because the setting sun and the array of sea-
weathered rocks, which were widely scattered across
the shore, provided me with a wealth of photographic
opportunity. It was an unexpected, but nonetheless
welcome, end to a cold and bracing winter day.

LEFT *Golden nuggets* **Near Llandanwg**

ABOVE *Sunset across Barmouth Bay* **Llandanwg**

ABOVE *A sliver of cloud* **Tremadog Bay**

Light and clouds play an important role in landscape photography and this means that
I spend a lot of time sky watching. It is not as tedious as it sounds and my thoughts, if
not my head, are often in the clouds. Occasionally, as I'm gazing upwards, the sky will
surpass itself and there are times when it deserves to be given centre stage and become
the main subject of the photograph. On the day I took this image dark rain clouds were
hovering behind me, in complete contrast to what I could see across the bay.

RIGHT *A celestial view* **Barmouth Bay**

When photographing the landscape I tend to lean towards minimalism. There is much to be said
for simplicity in composition and content. Here the crescent moon takes centre stage, supported
by a glowing twilight horizon. Additional elements are unnecessary, and indeed unwanted.

New Quay to St David's Peninsula

PREVIOUS PAGES *Church of the Holy Cross, late evening* **Mwnt**
Looking out across the Irish Sea and hidden away between Cardigan and Aberporth, Mynt
is a small, secluded cove with a clean, sandy beach and safe swimming. Such attractions are,
however, not my priority and it was the ancient chapel that attracted my attention. The present
building is thought to date back to the fourteenth century with the font pre-dating the main
structure, being twelfth century. A chapel has, though, occupied the site since the sixth century.

ABOVE *Cliff tops* **Aberporth**
With its two sheltered beaches, clean waters, safe swimming and cliff-top walks the
village of Aberporth has become a busy summer resort. It was once an important fishing
port, known for its herring catches, with over thirty fishing vessels based there by the 1830s,
but a fall in herring stocks led to the decline of the industry. Fishing still continues, particularly
for crab and lobster, but tourism is now Aberporth's main source of income.

ABOVE *A view worth climbing for* **Ceibwr Bay**

ABOVE *Pebbled beach* **Llangrannog**

Hidden away at the end of a minor, winding road, Llangrannog lies in an idyllic spot in one of the relatively few bays along the coastal stretch between New Quay and Cardigan. Its narrow, twisting street and colourful buildings give parts of the village a tranquil, olde worlde quality, and a sheltered beach with golden sands adds to its charm.

RIGHT ABOVE *Colourful cove* **Ceibwr Bay**

Ceibwr Bay is another remote and sheltered cove, which is often overlooked by the passing crowds. This is due to its relatively diminutive size and the presence of pebbles instead of sand. This is my kind of bay, pebbles and rocks offering more creative opportunity for image making than even the most golden stretch of beach.

RIGHT BELOW *Hidden jewels* **Ceibwr Bay**

PREVIOUS PAGES *The grand finale* **Strumble Head**
With its commanding view of the Atlantic Ocean Strumble Head is one of the best sites
in Britain to spot porpoises and seals. I didn't see any during my visit but I was, of course,
more concerned with the rapidly changing twilight sky. However, preoccupied as I was,
I chose my vantage point with care because this is an exposed and treacherously steep
headland. Stumble Head would perhaps be a more appropriate name for this rocky
headland and, windy as it is, it's possibly not the safest place for kite flying!

LEFT *Low sun, low tide* **Pwllgwaelod**

ABOVE *Spotlit cliffs* **Pwllgwaelod**
Tucked away at the end of a minor road is the tiny village of Pwllgwaelod. There
is not a lot there: just a car park, a café, a public house and a scattering of houses.
Apart from its charming location the main attraction is the sandy beach and the
marvellous view across Fishguard Bay. It's a perfect spot to watch the sun set –
as I discovered during my visit there one sunny October afternoon.

Fertile coastline **Newport**
As a rule I prefer not to photograph during the summer months. The quality of light
is not to my liking and popular destinations, particularly coastal resorts, are crowded
with people and cars, which I try not to include in my images. One benefit of
summer, however, is the coastal flora that flourishes at this time of year. It makes
an attractive subject and adds a dash of colour to the cliffs and rock faces.

A plethora of colours and textures **Newport Bay**
Wales is renowned for the variety of its coastline, but the rich diversity is due not only to
its size. Look carefully at any bay and you will discover a multitude of colours, textures,
shapes and patterns. From a distance Newport Bay is merely a sweeping expanse
of golden sand; closer inspection reveals a microcosm of graphic coastal features.

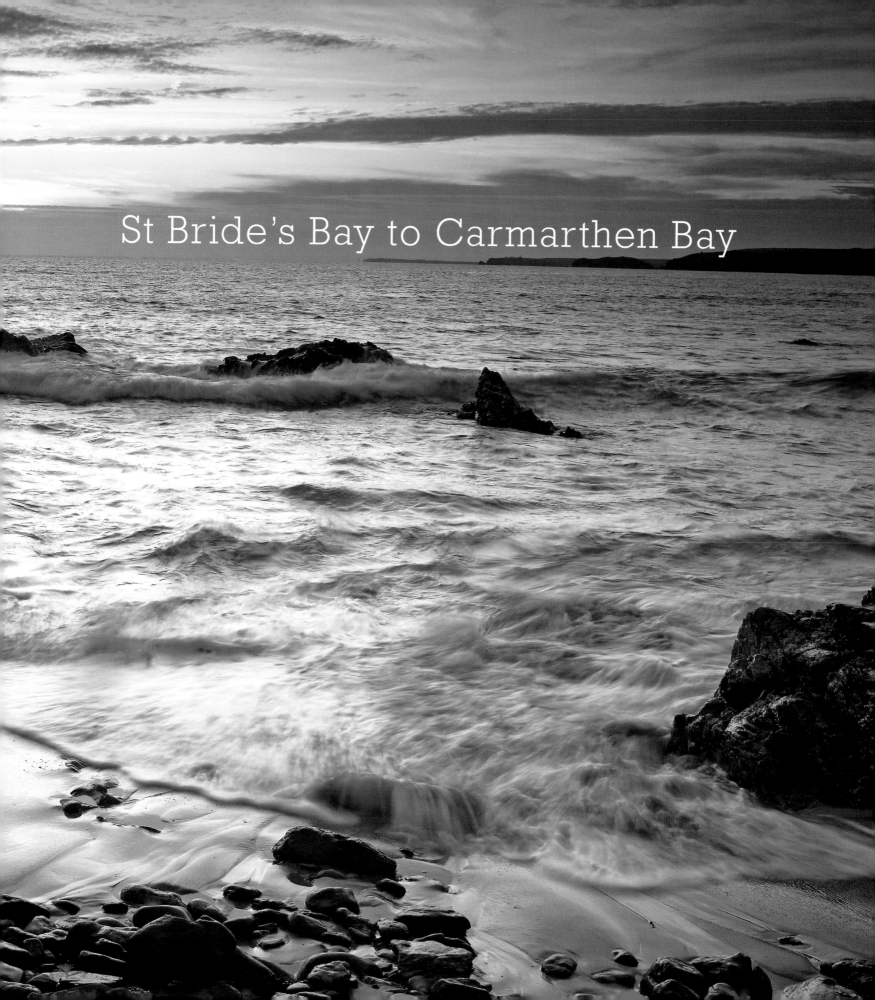

St Bride's Bay to Carmarthen Bay

PREVIOUS PAGES *Falling light, rising tide* **Freshwater West**

ABOVE *A colourful evening* **Westdale Bay, St David's Peninsula**
St David's is, geologically speaking, a tough peninsula. Its hard, igneous rock is able
to withstand the relentless pounding of the ocean waves and the abundance
of towering, sea-resistant cliffs has resulted in relatively few bays being formed
along this part of the coastline. However, what the area lacks in quantity is more
than compensated for in quality. Colourful, richly textured rocks and boulders
adorn the beaches and make fertile hunting ground for the hungry photographer.

RIGHT *Low tide at sunset* **West Angle Bay**

ABOVE *Deserted beach, midday, October* **Cwm-bach**
Next to Pwll March is Cwm-bach, a small bay accessible from the
beach only at low tide. Beyond the bay the Pembrokeshire coastal
path follows the course of the cliffs into the distance. For those
who enjoy an invigorating walk, taking an energetic hike along
the undulating path is a rewarding and exhilarating experience.

 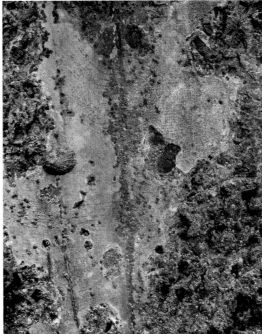 

LEFT ABOVE *Red sandstone* **Caerfai Bay**
Caerfai is an interesting and accessible bay with a number of rock pools and
caves to explore. The striking red stone is similar to that found at the neighbouring
Caerbwdy beach, from which St David's Cathedral was built during the twelfth
century. The presence of the cathedral earned the village of St David's city status
and, with a population of just 1800, it is, not surprisingly, the smallest city in Britain.

LEFT, BELOW LEFT *Rocky flora* **Little Furzenip**

LEFT, BELOW RIGHT *Rocky terrain* **Freshwater West**
Freshwater West is renowned for the quality of its surfing but it offers much more than
just water sports. This is a diverse stretch of coastline and its diversity extends to the
range of activities it supports. I visited the beach several times and, apart from the
surfing, there was always something else happening including fishing, kite flying,
dog walking, swimming (this is not for the fainthearted!) and of course, when I was
there, photography. All this activity along one beach and it wasn't even crowded.

ABOVE LEFT *Rugged cliff face and pebbles* **Pwll March**
Newgale is a 2-mile/3.2-kilometre stretch of sandy beach popular with holidaymakers
and water sports enthusiasts. The attractions for me, however, are the cliffs and
the enclosed bays at both ends of the beach. At the northern tip is Pwll March, an
Aladdin's cave of colourful rocks and intricately patterned stone, and of course a rich
source of images for the camera. I happily spent a day there foraging among the
boulders and rock pools and photographing the rich tapestry of coastal landscape.

ABOVE CENTRE *Weathered pipeline support* **Pembroke Dock**
A pipeline support is not, on the face of it, one of the coast's greatest attractions.
But add years of weathering and decay, and a transformation takes place. The steel
monstrosity gradually takes on a new appearance to become a plethora of rich
colours and rugged textures – the perfect raw material for striking abstract images.

ABOVE RIGHT *Precious gemstone rock* **The Towy Estuary**

LEFT *Rocks, boulders, cliffs* **Great Furzenip**

ABOVE LEFT *Water channel* **Freshwater West**

ABOVE RIGHT *Avenue of boulders* **Little Furzenip**

ABOVE *The highlight of the day* **West Angle Bay**

RIGHT *The beauty of dawn* **St Govan's Head**

View across the river from Pembroke Dock **Cosheston Point**

A magnificent display **Manorbier**

Did you know that there is a Cloud Appreciation Society? This admirable
organization was formed to recognize the importance and aesthetic qualities of
one of the world's natural wonders and, while I am not an active, paid-up member,
I take my hat off to the society for giving due recognition to a feature of the sky that
photographers generally consider to be an essential element in landscape images.
It was, in fact, the cloud formation that brought me to an abrupt and unexpected halt
as I drove along a quiet, coastal road. With camera and tripod set up in record time,
I wasted not a second in capturing the magnificent display. Clouds are ephemeral
and their position and shape was critical to the success of this image. Fortunately
it was a very calm day and I was able to make several exposures. I will be forever
thankful that I happened to be in the right place at the right time to photograph
the spectacle. It was a heaven-sent opportunity which I gratefully accepted.

The Gower Peninsula

PREVIOUS PAGES *Low tide, morning light* **Port Eynon Bay**

LEFT *Rugged terrain* **Mewslade Bay**

ABOVE LEFT *Precipitous cliffs* **Southgate**

ABOVE RIGHT *Photographer's paradise* **Mewslade Bay**

A glimpse of Weobley Castle **Landimore Marsh**
Along the Loughor Estuary, to the west of
Llanrhidian, is Landimore Marsh. Above the
marsh is a wooded cliff top known as Tor-gro.
This shelters the farmland lying behind it from
the gales that regularly sweep in from the
exposed estuary. Nestling among the trees, and
just visible on the horizon, is Weobley Castle.
The early history of the building is unclear,
but it is believed to have been constructed
in the eleventh or twelfth century. The origins
of Weobley village are more certain, it being
mentioned in the Domesday Book in 1086.

A fertile coastline **Llanrhidian Marsh**
The open spaces of Llanrhidian Marsh are where the rural countryside meets the coast. This vast expanse of fertile, flat land along the northern stretch of the Gower Peninsula is in stark contrast to the rugged, challenging coastline to the south. Llanrhidian holds no secrets; what it has it willingly reveals to even the most casual observer. You can take it all in with one sweeping view but this is not to its detriment. Indeed its open door is an invitation to wander through its tranquil plains and I have to admit that I found its lure compelling. This is a coastline where the seasons make a difference and the constantly changing appearance of the marsh is, for me, a source of inspiration and, of course, photographic opportunity.

ABOVE *Sea anemone, rockpool* **Slade Bay**
Underwater photography is not my field. I don't have the right
equipment or, indeed, the inclination to explore the aquatic depths.
Marine life is, however, a rewarding subject to study and rock pools can
be the source of many intriguing images. Here the depth of water is no
more than several inches, deep enough to support a sea anemone –
and shallow enough to keep photographer and camera dry!

RIGHT *Dramatic geology* **Port Eynon Bay**
The tiny village of Horton, on the far side of the beach, is dwarfed
by the dramatic and visually arresting geology of the rocky bay.

Winter sunrise **Port Eynon Bay**

Swansea to Cardiff

PREVIOUS PAGES *Discriminating light* **Rest Bay, Porthcawl**
Rest Bay lies at the southern end of a vast stretch of beach.
Its size means that it is never crowded, even during the peak
holiday season. This photograph was taken at the end of a
sunny October day when the beach was almost deserted.

LEFT *Rocky foreground, daybreak* **Mumbles Head**

BELOW *Cascading waters* **Dunraven Bay**

LEFT *Rock-pool microcosm* **St Donat's Bay**

I find it fascinating to study rock pools. These miniature, self-sufficient environments provide endless photographic opportunities and I never tire of crawling around and inspecting these tiny worlds. They are not particularly easy to photograph: the pools often lie in inaccessible places and reflections on the water's surface can be difficult to control. I don't want my photography to be easy, however: the greater the challenge, the greater the reward gained by eventual success.

ABOVE *Ocean froth* **Langland Bay**

Photographs often emerge from the unlikeliest origins. Here the combination of strong winds and an incoming tide has created sea froth and those tiny bubbles have acted as prisms in the low, morning sunlight. I got wet in the process of making this photograph (it took several attempts!) but it was, of course, worth every single wave-soaked splashing.

Molten rock **Dunraven Bay**

Cliff face **Dunraven Bay**

ABOVE *The Pavilion* **Penarth Pier**

At 650ft/198m Penarth pier is not particularly long, but that didn't prevent
it from being struck by the White Funnel paddle steamer Bristol Queen
in 1966. Prior to that unfortunate accident fire destroyed a substantial
part of the structure on a busy August bank holiday in 1931 and a major
rescue operation was mounted to evacuate the packed pier. In recent
years it has been returned to its former glory and become a popular
visitor attraction. The pier is open to the public throughout the year.

RIGHT *A splash of colour* **Ogmore-by-Sea**

There are impressive views to be enjoyed along the coast from the beach at
Ogmore. This, together with its caves and rock pools, make this an interesting
place to visit. Near by is Ogmore Castle. Built early in the twelfth century, during
the Norman invasion of Wales, the ancient monument, situated on the banks
of the River Ewenny, is rich in folklore and legend. Stepping stones lead across
the river from the castle grounds to the sprawling dunes of Merthyr-mawr.

FOLLOWING PAGES *A memorable moment* **Llantwit Major**

Acknowledgements

Producing the photographs for this book required careful planning and detailed organization. I wish to thank my daughter Sophie for managing my accommodation and travel arrangements as I journeyed along 1,700 miles (2,735 kilometres) of Welsh coastline. Her assistance was an invaluable aid and I am very grateful for the contribution she made to the completion of this book. I would also like to thank everyone at Frances Lincoln, particularly Maria Charalambous for creating the book's strong, eye-catching design.

LEFT *Rocky terrain* **Freshwater West**
RIGHT *Natural sculptures* **Mewslade Bay**
PAGE 111 *Fertile dunes* **Lligwy Bay**
PAGE 112 *A storm brewing* **Mumbles Head**

Index

The Welsh Coast

Isle of Anglesey

Dee Estuary

Llandudno

Holyhead

Conwy

Flint

Caernarfon

Lleyn Peninsula

Harlech

Aberystwyth

Aberaeron

New Quay

St David's

St Bride's Bay

Pembroke

Swansea

Newport

Carmarthen Bay

Cardiff

Gower Peninsula

N